It is important for us to not only ~~speak~~ our ~~truth~~ ~~but~~ ~~listen~~ to
the truths of others. In 2018, I sta~~rted~~ an ~~open~~ mic ~~in~~ my ~~classroom~~ for
that purpose. Each month, students would share their writing about
topics that were important to them. Be it depression, racism, or issues
with schoolwork or friends, they learned they were not alone. New
friendships were born. Confidence in their writing and sharing their
voice grew each time they stepped to the microphone.

And then the world was struck with a pandemic and school as we
knew it changed. BARZ & Noble went weekly and virtual. Their
words, written in the form of poetry, became a focus of our online
classroom. Poetry gave my students a way to write their way through
a difficult time while also providing a window into their experiences.
Some of those writings are found in this book.

Please enjoy the gift of poetry these students are giving you. And as I
say to them at the end of each class: "Go forth, have a great day, and
do something nice for someone!"

Smiles,

Mandie Robertson

Special Thanks

Church da Poet
We had a vision of what could happen when you give kids a microphone. Little did we know how it would grow.

Clifton Thomas
Always supportive with each poet I brought into the classroom.

Dragon Team Teachers – Kent Lewis, Felix Flanders, Roseanna Morgan, Laurence Isaccs
You supported me and even stepped to the mic on occasion.

Wendy Jones
Without whom this book wouldn't have been made.

City Soul Café Open Mic
The inspiration behind it all.

Feature Poets

Each month well-known poets came to BARZ & Noble Classroom Open Mic. They gave us the gift of their poetry and listened to the students as they shared their truths. A very special thank you to the feature poets that stepped up to the mic.

Main Man

Lady Dope

Queen Prophet Sage

Tim Jackson

Raven Herndon

Dasan Ahanu

Kimberly Gaubault

Suave the Poet

Jimmy Free Love

Sh8kes

Ajani Kambon

Langston Fuze

Tr1umphant

Endless Will

Spoken Watson

Dr. Storm

Cortland Gilliam

DJ Rogers

Kandice Corbett

Breeze the Poet

Sergio

Matthew Cuban Hernandez

Law Bullock

Azar King

Lavinia "Missie"Jackson

Clarity

S.p.

POETS

Leslee Moore

Haley Boyden

Jorden Davis

Amir Hester

Darryn Johnson

Myshaun Stanback

Nolan Sulyans

Aldo Arroyo-Arroyo

Kimberly Cortez

Abbie Deskins

Mia MyLychok

Trenton Hayes-Roberts

Sky Williams

Tatyana Cheek

Maddy Wykle

Ella Williams

Sarah Rodrigues

Soffie Suarez

Amir Gowdy

Permelia Omuchei

Joshua Kiplagat

Dominic Pedde

Meredith Plemmons

Ruby Stinett

Deasya Walker

Tasia Washington

Nicole Argueta-Medina

Alia Bell

Mei Brown

Aiden Zeininger-Dick

The Start of a Life-Changing Spring Break

Leslee M

I will never forget the day they told us that were having a early spring break

We had to get ready for a special visitor

It was on Friday March 13, 2020

The principal told us that we needed time to plan for our visitor from China

Families had to go shopping for food, water,and any needed items

They told us that we were coming back to school in a few weeks

Spring break ended, and we returned to school but online

Going to school online was very different

I researched the visitor's name, and it was Coronavirus 19 or better known as COVID-19

COVID-19 was not very friendly

It made us stay inside locked up or what they call "quarantine"

This quarantine has lasted for almost two months

To make matters worse, they told us last week

That we are not going back to the DSA campus for the rest of the school year

Thousands of people have died from COVID-19

Some People look at the death rate like its just a number

But its not just numbers that we are talking about

These are actual people

They had lives

They had families

And they had friends

Look how many people lost their jobs

Look at how many people are worrying about how they are going to pay for rent

Or how they are going to feed their kids

We should be working together to fight this pandemic

But as I look around, some people are just selfish

They are not following instructions and putting others at risk

Some people are turning this situation in to a political war

Politicians should be looking out for their citizens and not for themselves

We need to come together

Protect one another

Wear a mask

Respect physical distance

Wash and sanitize your hands

Lastly, we should have hope and eat birthday cake

So, we do not have to experience another quarantine spring break

Life and it's changes!

Haley

Life is a complicated thing

and it can lead to many things

like getting your boss to say yes

to a book you want to get published.

And then there is when you have lost a loved one

or just got fired from your only job that will accept you.

As you think about what you did wrong and why it happened,

you can't help but think why…...

why do I have to be this way?

Why did I make all of those stupid mistakes

that caused so many other people pain.

As you think bad and look down on yourself,

you think you don't matter in this world.

 Life is like a black hole just waiting to suck you up in two seconds

and take you into nowhere

where you can't see your parents or loved ones or even talk to them.

It is like a living Hell in this cycle that is going to

keep on going forever and ever and never stop.

Most books have a happy ending, right?

No, I'm tired of pretending that life is perfect

because it is not.

Take a moment to stop pitying yourself

you will see how we made this world a horrible place to live in.

maybe the reason why we are so unhappy most of the time is

 because of the way we make the world out to be.

If we make the world out to be a bad disgusting polluted place

then it will be a bad disgusting polluted place.

It is a little too late to make some of the changes

I want in the world

but most of them can be fixed

I hope all of you can try to make an effort to make a change too.

Fortnite

JoWitDaJuice (Jorden)

My mom won't give me her card for Fortnite

Because she says her money is too tight

I just want to stay up all night

So I can get elims in a box fight

Trying to win skins in the battle pass

While building boxes around my enemies, kid you're trash!!

Please mom can I get your card

Because these wins are getting hard.

Stuck Inside

Amir H.

When you've been stuck inside,

it gets boring.

You can only watch Netflix for so long.

All I did was listen to music

and play Fortnite.

Now it's getting boring.

I'm ready to go back to school

and do something.

It's just so boring!

So I'm writing

how I feel in this poem.

Being home is boring

and kind of fun.

"Why Me"

Darryngokrazy (Darryn)

You are the world to me,

 I don't know if other people see it.

Out of all the other boys you picked me.

Why me?

What did I do to make you feel the way you do about me?

I just wonder...

Why me?

You had all these other options,

but you chose me.

I am not special,

and my personality is terrible.

So why did you pick me?

What do you see in me that you don't see in other boys?

Is it my looks?

Or the way I speak?

Is it the way I treat you?

Or the way you see me?

Umm...I think I know!

It's because I'm different.

Nah, I don't think it's that...never mind.

You say that I say different things than other boys

and that you trust me.

That must be why me.

My Three Favorite Holidays
Myshaun

CHRISTMAS

a day of peace,

a day when people sing carols,

one of the days where snow is there.

On Christmas there could be snowball fights,

or hot chocolate.

You can also sit by the fire.

Family and Friends are the main part of Christmas.

Christmas was even the day my baby brother was born.

THANKSGIVING

a day where families come together,

have a big feast,

and maybe even stay with each other for a few days.

On Thanksgiving, you can have anything to eat like

seafood, pizza, turkey, vegetables, and other meals.

Thanksgiving is always about family.

ST.PATRICK'S DAY

a leprechaun's birthday,

where you have to wear green

otherwise you will get pinched.

On this holiday you can have meals

with your friends and family,

have fun with them,

and pinch each other all night.

My Hopes for Drawing
Nolan

Hope is when you see a bright light inside your heart
Hope is the result of being embraced like this pencil that I hold
in my grip
As I sit under the tree an ant was just crawling on my pencil
The ant would think it was a tree breezing in the wind but
instead,
It is the momentum of my pencil

Filled with power me drawing like the breezing wind flowing
I would put my hand to potential and I would take my time
drawing like a steady turtle
My art is like the beauty of a Macaw I can see the reflection of
colors in my artwork
Made to display the beauty of the rain forest leaving me
dumbfounded

The colors swirling in delight like a bird circling in flight
The colors were like a panther chameleon shining bright, Oh so
bright!
My hand roaring with confidence and power as a lion that
attacks its prey
No different then Coronavirus has torn our community apart
today
My hopes of drawing have increased, as we separate in our
social distancing.

Power
Aldo

Power
What is power?
Power is something you have,
Something we all have,
We could use it anytime of day.
You could use it in a good, or bad way…
No matter how we use it,
we all have it.
So, be proud,
be excited,
be happy,
that power is within you!

Silent
The Silent Angel (Kimberly)

The silence
It surrounds me
No matter how much I want it to stop
But whatever
Cause they HATE me
Forever
I don't know why?
But they do
I see the people
I Love
Turn into ASH
More hatred
Blooms
Just like flowers
But worse than flowers
Seconds turn into Minutes
Minutes turn into Hours
Hours turn into Days
Days turn into Months
Then Months turn into Years
No matter what
I am surrounded by silence

Everything Changed
(A poem for two voices)
Abbie and Soffy

You said I was strong,
but you shut me out.

You said I could do anything,
but you let me down

I hide myself away from you
to ensure sure you're happy too.

I feel all alone when I'm with you,
a cloud of rain in a dark room.

How do you feel when I'm with you?
Do you see that same Dark Room?

You said we were best friends till the end,
but we don't see that light anymore.

I scream and shout and try to soar,
but now we can't see the trust anymore.

You made me feel like I was bound
to the friendship we had before.

A fairy tale without a happy ending.
The only thing happy about it was the beginning

<u>Expectations</u>
Taskmaster (Amir G)

Sometimes...
I feel like nothing gets better
and the people around me
get stressed.
I try to tell them
I'm doing my best,
but my best is not enough.
I know
they are not trying to be tough on me.
Sometimes...
I don't meet their expectations,
but I will soon enough.

STOP!
Permelia

Stop!
Stop bullying!
Stop making people feel less of themselves
If they feel the world would be a better place if we just stop
doing certain things.
They are the people and the society
we need to listen to the people .
And we need to learn how to listen to these people cause we
don't.
We listen to the millionaires that try so hard to relate to us
like you really don't
when you reach the top of the mountain you never wanna
come down.
when you look the "prettiest " out of all the girls in the room
you'd never wanna come down to "those girls in the room"
if we are too fat in the eyes in the people
we need to become skinny, go on a treadmill - like that's gonna
help at all
if we're too skinny we need to eat a burger
and get a little bit of more human flesh put on our upset bodies
.

We make arguments of who should say a word
that was so hurtful to many blacks back in the day
that made them feel so owned by horrible smug people that
might be your ancestor
or the slave that might be my ancestors.
The people should stop
I'm not going to take one group out of the human race and
blame it on them
why because what I'm saying wouldn't make sense
because I'm putting my opinion over others.
this place we call home needs help locking kids and parents in
cages like they're some type of animal or a rag doll.

We tell people who they're allowed to love. A girl can't like a
girl.
A boy can't like a boy because it's not normal in society's eyes.
What does normal mean to you cause I've never met a normal
person.
Normal is boring meaningless
to be honest I'd hate being normal.
STOP!
Stop bullying!
Stop making people feel less of themselves!
Stop what you call normal isn't normal for the world!
STOP!

Music
Dominic

Helps me focus while I work
It calms me down
Songs make me feel sad but also happy
Music helps me doze off on sleepless nights
It entertains me in the car when I have nothing to do

BOOM!
Meredith

Boom
A crash to my left
Boom
I can feel a wave surrounding me
The wind becomes harsher with every breath I take
I look up and can feel the wave breathing on me
BOOM

The wave has crashed
I am now breathing easy

Time
Ruby S.

The time ticks by everyday
There is never one moment where the time just stops but in our
mind it does.
See when time stops for us, we get lost in our minds,
Thinking of unicorns and dragons and just knowing they are
real.
We just have this thought in our minds that brings us into a
whole new world.
Sometimes we get a little bit too lost that we start sleeping in
class and having a dream about flying and having super
powers.
Sometimes it's okay to get lost in your head because you think
of new ideas and you have a way more creative mind set.
Right when you wake up from your eyes wandering around the
classroom an hour went by and you don't know what
happened.

Untitled
DeAsya

The rain, pain, the grief and glory.
You feel wasted like you don't mean anything to the world
you think of the negatives and not the positive.
You're in the dark every morning until 2 in the afternoon
barely even moving.
Waiting for that person to come and get you
to say, "I got you."
It makes you feel special
like you're a part of something.
You're not an outcast
because people actually want you around.
They want to see your smile in the morning.

The Fire Alarm
Tasia

Falling asleep or waking up.
 Either one can be a struggle.
 A dream or a nightmare.
 People can be in their own bubble.
Sleep is a different state than anything coming first-hand or
second-rate.
When sleeping everything comes light-weight.
All that is loud and noisy manifests and becomes pearls and
diamonds,
and all that is nice and sweet becomes dangerous and pointy.
 Full of joy like a vivid rainbow.
I watch them laugh and they cry hello.
Everyone has promises to keep,
sweet dreams comes to some cheap.
The only other sounds of distant blades and birds awake.
Some sob until the tars break.
Lie in bed with cuts and ducts that weep.
 Idolizing life with never-ending dread for the day ahead.
Although those who had been granted life
make it their short-life goal for their eyes to be closed forever;
not having to hear their head.

{ Sorry for the sadness }

Memories
Nicole

Memories. The things we hold close.
The things we smile and cringe at.

Those awkward times we are told to forget
because "They won't matter later," or because
"They were just moments meant to stifle your
success,".
Why are we told to forget about it when we cant
or told to stop thinking about it when it's
burned deep into our minds?

Why are we told to leave behind the things
you have preached for us to keep and
cherish?
Why are we told to forget the moment that we
remember more than what happened on
January 16 of 2012?

Why are we told to forget something we carry
with us like a heavy bowl of water?
A heavy bowl of water you're bringing home in a drought.
These are our memories.

These are the things we hate and love more than
we can even realize.
These are the fragments of time we will remember
for days to come.

And the words you have read now drift away from
those memories.
And you're left with the message of
the simple words on this piece of paper.

Just these very words are now prominent in your
mind, ready to be remembered.
But soon they will be faded in your own thoughts
caused by the complex concept of what we call memories.

The Calling From The Sky
Sunflower (Alia)

Rain poured.
I heard it scream as it hit the ground.
I watched it walk down to my neighbors home.
It poured so badly it covered the gray pavement.
It was like it was calling to me.
It was almost as if it was trying to tell me something.
But what?
It cried but only I heard.

My Name Is
Mei Lin

May you always remember the name.
May you remember the breath that you breathe from your lungs
as it comes out of your mouth when you say,
Mei.
May the sound of my middle name bring you to the petals of a
flower similar to that of the mythical ancient lotus,
And may my first name bring the love felt by a family in arms
reach
Mei Lin.
There are many ways to interpret the syllables of my name
written and spoken in Cantonese.
The beautiful notes in my name, harmonize with the way they
are spoken
It is an insult to me, my parents, and my unfinished legacy,
When you mispronounce the lyrics to a song called Mei Lin.
My name is
M-E-I
L-I-N
The M is for the Magic that is me.
E stands for Eva, the person I could have been.
I stands for the Intelligence that I hold, and will hold
The L is for the mythical flower, Lin, my middle-name's
namesake
I stands for my Imagination, when I weave together letters in
the stories I tell
My N stands for the Nobility that I hold in my actions and
words.
My name,
Is Mei Lin,
May you never forget it.

I Believe
Aiden

I believe
But what do I believe
Do I believe in myself
Do I believe in others
No
I believe that
People keep telling me
To believe
But I can't
How do I believe
Whenever one of my friends
Are doing something
Competitive
And we need to cheer for them
And I say that
I believe in them
I don't mean it
No not like that
I mean that
I shouldn't have to believe
Shouldn't they already know
That I believe in them
Because I'm their friend
And I'll support them
No matter what
So I don't know why I'm
Believing
It doesn't make sense
To me
I'm confused

When I say that I
Believe in them
It's more of a motivational phrase
Whenever I try to believe
I think of all the other times
When I tried to believe and it hurt
Then I start to hurt
It just hits me
I feel like I just got punched
In the gut
I feel sick now
I can't do it
I have to stop
But my friends
I said I'd support them
No matter what
What will they do
But they should know
That I believe in them
Even if I don't show it
But what if they don't
What if they don't know the way
That I do things
How I live
Then they'll for sure be mad
Maybe they won't care
Maybe they'll just forget it
I think all that I have to do is believe
That my friends will believe
That I believe in them
But if i believe that
Then this cycle of me
Getting hurt from believing
Will just start all over again

Untitled
Beef Jerky (Martin)

A brick wall lies in my way.

Nature's creation, our creation, lies in my way.

It knows how I need to advance forward, and is just staying here, making me climb over it, making the illusion my wall of anxiety is larger compared to my society.

The wool has been pulled over my eyes for too long now.

What masterful mastermind is behind this film, obscuring my vision of an existence in which I can finally be satisfied?

Maybe I can shatter the wall, and collapse my fears. I bet a natural hand can break some natural minerals.

Who knows how powerful my spirit truly is?

...I shouldn't have tried punching it.

Who knew I'd wake up the next morning with my aching body, limbs, head and fractured right-hand knuckles?

Broke my wrist.

I feel a stinging pain surging through my body to my hopeless brain, frying its mainframe.

My new brain, a scrambled egg, sunny side up, is complete with a medium-sized organic glass of anxiety.

The anxiety is delicious, nutritious and intentionally malicious.

Why do I think that I'm not very strong, to react to pain this way?

I stare at the wall.

With its bricks in a certain formation, it taunts me with an inanimate smirk.

It's as if my fears are as human as I am, the wall is as human as I am...

But humans don't aim to aggravate each other...is that true?

The wall feeds me bitter doubt through my nerves.

I just turned 12 years old today, what's with these fears treating me like I'm weak and incapable of thriving in this surreal existence known as the third dimension, this society we call our Earth?

I guess I can't complain about the truth.

I just want to go home, and shred the wrapping paper off my presents, as if I'm a workaholic composer with songwriter's block, tearing up thousands of pages of sheet music.

My masterpiece is cacophonic, but the fragments of paper conceal a treasure greater than music.

I just want to go home, and hear my family sing the most beautiful song, the song that is impossible to replicate to produce more positivity from others, the song that makes the candles on the birthday cake grow with excitement, for the music is so euphonious, it's cheerful

To the ears of even the most disrespectful people on the dark side of your own Earth.

I just want to go home, and smell the aroma of dark chocolate seeping off of the fluffy, triple-layered cake.

I want to taste the richness that comes from the inner layer, and I know that nobody in the room would avoid licking the creamy frosting off of their own fingers.

This obstacle does not understand. My home, my life is behind you.

I want to go home to see my family. I want to lay down under the stars at twilight, without a care in the world.

Every year I age leaves me less and less innocent. Every year marks the increase of my maturity, although I'm not even close to mature. The number ages, my lifetime decreases.

Why won't this wall let me live my life to the best? Why is it stopping me from living a life clear of responsibility? Or, is it just preparing me for the worst parts of my life, when I'm older.

But who cares if I have fears? Why should I care? I'm not scared to be scared.

Who made this thing? Nature created this, we created this, but nature didn't intend to create it.

However, we did.

All I truly need to know is what is beneath the wrapping paper. I think it's a gift card.

How does knowing that the mitochondria is the powerhouse of the cell, or the area of a circle help my future?

It's for the greater good, but I'm still climbing this tall wall made of bricks.
I'll call it school.
Sounds kind of fitting.

A Hero
Ellie H

A hero is...it is...well what is a hero?
We keep talking about the heroes of our country but most of
them are white heroes?
The black heroes are few but are they heroes?
I mean, you don't see them planting more trees, do you?
But we don't see white heroes doing much either.
But maybe to find the real heroes you just have to look around.
Did you see the new saplings in the fun lunch area?
Or how crossing guards help seniors across the street?
I guess to find the real heroes, you just have to look around and
in the mirror.
You may think that there is nothing you can do.
Sometimes being a hero means admitting you were wrong.
Because you too can be a hero.

i write on the wall
ellie I.

i write on the wall
my true thoughts
my true feelings
i am anonymous, like a traveler
always moving yet always leaving a mark
i write on the wall in a strange place
no one will know who wrote on the message on the wall
no one will know who made the thick sharpie lines
that pop against the white brick in front of me
but they will all read the message:
ONLY U KNOW U
just like only i know that i wrote on the wall
only i will know the true meaning of what i wrote
did i just write it or did it mean something?
ask me, but you can't
i didn't listen to my own advice i wrote on the wall all those
years ago
i let other people tell me who i am
now i am no longer me, i am who they told me to be
now i don't even remember that i wrote on the wall
…
a long time passed
i lived my life trapped
i could not remember who i was
i was who they wanted me to be
then i went back to a place that was not unknown
i went back to where i wrote on the wall
 i didn't know that was where i wrote on the wall
but i read the message, just like anyone else
it seemed to spark something
i seemed to remember
i only remembered i thing, but that 1 thing was all i needed

i remembered

i
wrote
on
the
Wall

The Past
Frisk (Chloe)

We can't predict the future, no matter how hard we try
The past we can dodge
Like bullets raining down on a stormy day
As if it were lava in your Minecraft world
It's harder than you think though
Think of the past as...a boomerang!
It stays away when you throw it, but always returns later
It'll come back to haunt you
Especially if your past isn't very pleasant…
But, alas, the harder you throw it, the longer it'll stay away
It takes an amount of energy as big as the SUN to keep it away
That's why we throw it often or try and dodge it
To hold onto it could be harder in some cases
Others might have thrown theirs
Seeing yours wouldn't be the best thing…
I should know
That's exactly how I ended up here
In a huge mountain
On a flower patch 200 feet underground
Nobody for miles
I have no choice but to throw my boomerang now
tosses nothing Should be back in a month or so
Welp, time to figure out where I am
I just hope I don't die…
But before I go,
Ask yourself one thing:
"Where is my boomerang?"
You might just find out something you never knew
About yourself
Not anyone else. YOU.
Well, here I go!

I'm Lost
Lucy

I'm lost
I know my coordinates, but I'm lost
I have a map
but I'm lost
I know north, south, east, and west
but I'm lost
I see the start, I know the finish
but I'm lost
Who knows what the light at the end of the tunnel is
Is it the sun
Shining beams of hope, joy, and freedom
Or a coming train
That carries anxiety, frustration, and misconception
If the tunnel is just in my head....
Then it must never end
It would loop out one ear and come right back in the other
I'm lost
In emotion
In confusion
In myself worries and doubts
But for now, if I can't find a way to dig deeper, I'm lost
And so many others are lost in the same mind
turny, twisty, boggling tunnel
But we're too caught up in ourselves to notice everyone around
us
Maybe that's why I'm lost

Word
Sarah

You thought about it
I know you did
I saw you hesitate before saying it
and yet you still did
you filled the gun of your vocal cords
with new poisonous ammo
and you shot
you aimed you shot and you hit
hit me in the head with your searing hot bullet
it struck through my head and stayed there
floating in my brain
slowly eliminating each and every one of my memories
for a second, I stood there half-dead
forgetting how to breathe
how to function correctly
then I'm okay
well I am physically okay
but my mind was still a void of darkness with a single gray
thought inside
it would have been just as dark, but the bullet and the gun
wanted me to be able to see it
to be reminded of it
so there it was dark and foggy but still visible
but this, this wasn't what bothered me most
what bothered me most is that you were my friend
at least up until this
but you still thought we were friends
you still thought we were friends because you said that this was
a joke
but it wasn't
because I could see the flame in your eye before you said it
that flame meant it

that flame meant every single word that burst out of your
mouth
and now here you are drenching the flame with water hoping to
extinguish it, to hide the evidence,
to cover it up
you said it was just a joke
but you saying that didn't extinguish the flame
it didn't erase or cover up the fact
that you shot your friend.

The Right Path
Ella

There's a road we all walk on
A set path we are told to follow
It's a straight line
Moving forward with certainty
But what happens when you break off
When you wander into the woods of the unknown around you
You are all alone
No support or guidance from peers
In fact, most people on the straightforward road peek through
the dense jungle surrounding you
Just to stare and laugh at the outcast who will never go
anywhere in life

It's a difficult journey
You get cut and scarred from the sharp obstacles that lie before
you
And at one point
It is finally too much
The underbrush in front of you is to big to scale or go around
So you sit in despair and watch all the people walking down
that straight away path
"If only I had gone that way"
you think
And it seems like the only logical way is to turn back
Go and follow the crowd
Be like everyone else
But just when you thought you were a nobody
And everyone else had chosen the better option
You remember that you were the one with the grand idea
And you are gonna stick with it
No matter how deep the cuts or big the bruises

So you fight through the problem
And finally, you are free
Continuing on, you realize the path is straighter than before
And before you know it
You are out of the woodland
Your perseverance finally paid off
People surround you asking for pictures and signatures
You are welcomed to a stage to win an award
And in the sea of unfamiliar faces
You find the nosebleeds, filled with the gazing eyes of all the unbelievers
The ones who spoke about you in only gossip and giggles
And before you even know what to think
The mic is passed to you
You are expected to boast about the glass statue in your hand
Instead, you tell a simple quote
One that sums your decades of effort in eleven words
"No one ever made a difference, by being like everyone else"
-P.T. Barnum

Pen And Paper
Biscotti (Sky)

Pen and paper
Both together
Separated so many times
But it comes back together
As if it's now or never
Or as if, one of them will die
Dogs and cats
Love's like a gnat
Still kinda in the air
But to be fair
Their friendship took some time, somewhere
A fish and water
Never separated
Or one of them will die
The water would swell up and cry and cry
As the fish was one of a kind
Me and you
Here again
Trying to show me your love
Telling you "No,
That I don't need your love."

Sunflower
Tatyana

I bloom as the sun hits my petals
The ray of the sun exfoliates my bright yellow wings
I feel like flying but my roots are stuck
But if you pull me out
I'm sure to die
I'm a delicate little flower
Just let me be, in peace do I rest
Let's not be crazy

Untitled
Trenton

It a big world around us,
we are like little mice looking for cheese
Instead, we are looking for things to help us live in this big
earthy ball,
because we need that knowledge to survive this maze of life.
Life is a big movie, but you are the main actor.
"As a baby you have a diaper full of dreams," said the character
from the Rugrats.
Those dreams could be the next cure for the coronavirus
or next in line to be Kobe Jr, boy or girl,
It doesn't matter what people say about your spirit of your life,
You are the head of your movie.
Don't let people bring your idea down,
they are just mad that you are making mill for your coronavirus
cure.
Follow your dreams,
not the big world around us.

To Be Human
Mia

To be human it means you are special.
 You are different from other animals.
Humans are great and all, but we need
to remember we are not alone on earth.
People come in all shapes and sizes,
some people judge other people by
what they look like.
Please DON'T do that.
It is not at all kind.
Remember we are all humans.
Wonderful humans.

Far Star
Ruby M.

Breathing slowly in the farthest corner of the earth's vision,
alone and excluded from the days down below her,
lies the farthest star from the rest.
Unseen and sad, she cries above the moon.
Her tears slowly began to crystallize
as they fall slowly one by one down her cindered and cracked
face.
She looks for a friend but no one's there...
not even the sun acknowledges her presence.
Some days she wishes she could just fall from the vast sky
and join the mesmerizing sea of joyful people below on earth.
Alone and feeling useless
she lies as her tears turn to sobs
that then turn to a long cold bitter silence.

<u>Love Letter</u>
Merlina

A letter to you my love
the things that I love about you...
The things that give you the reason I love you my dear.
When you smile,
I feel safe and happy that you see me as the person you love.
When we hold each other's hands,
your warmth is so powerful I want to hug you
so much to show you I love you
and your personality is so cute it drives me crazy.
It's so pretty.
When the day comes,
I will give you a ring that shows the promise
you made when we first met
and the love you give me
and the purpose to live with you.
Thank you, my love.

The Mess
Maddy

Why are humans so dumb?
We spread diseases
We've ruined earth
If we find another place, we'll probably destroy that one, too
We're trying to revive it,
 but not everyone is helping
The next generation will be cleaning up our mess.
We believe our president will fix this,
but what he is doing is building a wall to keep other humans
out.
Do you know, my mind is made up on which path the world
must take,
But is your mind made up?

Quarantine
Aiden Z.

Quarantine is so boring.

Staring at the ceiling for hours.

I can't even move anymore.

Doing 4 zoom meetings a day.

I SPEND half of my day going to zoom meetings.

I have to SIT HERE AND LISTEN TO MY SISTER list off things you can put cheese on.

Cheese on carrots,

cheese on strawberries,

cheese on cake,

cheese on apples,

cheese on chocolate,

cheese on cheese…...

ok I think you get the point now.

You feel my pain, right?

The days keep dragging on like math homework.

I can not wait until all this virus stuff goes away.

Because you can do whatever you want at that point.

Everything will open back up

and we will be like a herd of wildebeests running towards shopping malls, restaurants, and...everything.

We'd be crazy.

Because we have been stuck in our houses for an eternity.

I never thought I would say this,

I want to go back to school.

<u>Coronavirus</u>
Anderson K.

Quarantine, Wuhan, Coronavirus,

That's all we hear now.

But some people hear:

YOU caused coronavirus,

YOU have to wear a mask.

I get looked at like I am the virus itself.

Just going for a walk seems like a nightmare,

 when the so few people outside stare at you like you are the enemy,

that minuscule monster lurking in the depths.

I don't care I'm Asian,

that I caused coronavirus,

I wasn't even born in China.

Some people see me and think that,

but I don't care what they think or what they believe,

because they don't know me,

or who I am.

I am Phenomenally Asian,

 I'm proud that 75% of my family is from Asia,

It's Phenomenal to be me,

to be who I am right now.

I Have it Easy
Anonymous

I have it easy

I'm not sick

I'm not hungry

My parents still have jobs

I have three devices all to myself

Because of this I'm sometimes blind

Blind to what is happening

Unaware of the people that are dead

I don't want to be blind

I want to care. I do care

But sometimes I try and I can't

My vision is fogged over

I'm scared of small things

Things that don't matter

I have it easy

Yeah I'm bored

Yeah I'm stuck in my house

But I have it easy

In times I am rolled up in my own fears

Fears that are unimportant to so many out there

Fears that make it hard to see

Problems that make me blind

I try to forget my petty problems and see those that are struggling

Those that have real problems

I know I have it easy

That makes me blind

But it also does the opposite

It helps me see

There is a war in my head

A war between my fading vision and how I want to see the world

I have it easy

I'm sometimes blind

But I want to see

And that's all I hope people ask of me

Letter to My Students
Mandie R.

Dear students past and present

My time in the classroom is coming to an end. After 27 years spanning two countries and three states, September of 2020 I will be traveling down the road less taken.
I am not just going to drop that on you, give you a hug, and wish you much happiness in life and be on my way.
Nah, I am going to leave you with a bit of what I learned about life while teaching all of you.

It is lessons outside of the textbook that I wish to review one more time

Spend time reading
Read for the joy of it - to escape into another world for awhile, to learn something new, to walk in the shoes of another
Just read

Never stop writing
The words inside of you are important
Whether it is to remember a moment in time, let someone know you appreciate them, or let the struggle happening inside seep out through the ink onto paper - write
You have a story to tell

Use your voice
No matter how shaky it is, speak your truth.
What you have to say is important.
Like any other muscle, the more you use it, the stronger it gets.
Your voice has power.
Speak up for others when their words can't be found.

There is magic in combining your writing and voice
Use the power of spoken word to share your struggles and celebrations.
Speak those BARZ and be noble
Your voice will be heard and will merge with the unspoken words of those who are not yet ready to speak their truth.

Have the tough conversations with people not like you
Gender, age, race, religion, sexual identity, living situation
Whatever the difference, listen and ask questions.
Like Really listen and learn from what you hear.
Take it in and change your behavior accordingly

If you mess up - and you will
Give yourself permission to fail.
Own it, apologize if need be, and know that failure is nothing more than a lesson.
An opportunity to reflect and find another way.
It will make you stronger, smarter, and a better human if you let it.

Whatever you are going through, you are not the only one.
Failure, mental illness, death of a loved one, poor choices, bad grades, sexual assault, figuring out your identity, anxiety about what is happening in the world...or your neighborhood,
or something else altogether.
Whatever it is, you are not alone.
Let me repeat that one...you are not alone.
When you are struggling and need help -
Reach out.
Ask for help
There is power when we figure it out together

The only right way to do life is to live it.
YOU always have the choice.
Others may not agree with it, take their counsel and decide what is best for you.

Sometimes you will make a poor choice, learn from it.
Use it to become a better version of you.
You may not be ready to live your choice. Hold on to it. You
will know when the time is right to make your move.
Know that you have the power to be who you want to be.
The choice is yours.
Choose wisely.

From that first moment you walked into my classroom, whether
I taught you or not, you became one of my kids.
No matter how old you get or where your journey takes you,
you will always have a piece of my heart.
Oh, and a quick reminder - you are never too old for hugs.

It has been an honor to teach every single one of you.
As our time comes to an end, I say to you one more time
"Go forth, have a great day, and do something nice for
someone."

Made in the USA
Columbia, SC
11 July 2020